Brown Thrashers   *at Their Twig Nest*

BIRDS
IN THEIR HOMES

PICTURES BY SABRA MALLETT KIMBALL
TEXT BY ADDISON WEBB

DOUBLEDAY & COMPANY, INC.
GARDEN CITY, N. Y.

The Northern Yellow-Throat

Contents

Introduction   3

The Smallest Bird   5

Springtime and Mud Nests   9

Birds That Build with Twigs   15

Birds That Use Grasses   21

Birds That Like to Use Hair   29

Birds That May Be Seen in the Snow   32, 33

Birds That Nest in Holes   37

Bird Houses and Birds That Will Live in Them   40, 41

Birds That Nest in Holes in the Ground   45

The Parasite Bird   47

Suspended Nests   49

No Nests and Seashore Nests   57

Alphabetical Index of the Birds in This Book   66

Introduction

Some birds live under the ground.

Others live high up in the trees.

Some build their homes with mud.

Others like to make homes of grasses or of hair,

   or of sticks and stones.

If they don't know how to build a nest

   they may use a convenient hole,

   or dig one themselves

   or just choose a spot on the bare ground.

For all birds have to find a place

   to raise their families.

The Smallest Bird

THE
RUBY-THROATED HUMMINGBIRD

The Ruby-throated Hummingbird is one
   of the smallest birds in the world.

Its wings beat so fast that they make a humming noise.

That is how the Hummingbird got its name.

This tiny bird looks something like a large Bumble bee
   as it hovers around the flowers.

It feeds on the honey that lies deep in the center
   of the brightly colored blossoms.

The Ruby-throat likes best, red or orange flowers
   such as those of the trumpet vine in this picture.

The nest of the Hummingbird is a lovely

little cradle lined with plant down.

The inside is soft and warm.

The outside is covered with lichens

held together with spiderweb.

Lichens grow on the bark of trees.

For that reason, a nest built with lichens

looks like part of the tree.

The Hummingbird generally builds its nest

in an orchard out on a small limb.

It lays two eggs.

The eggs are white in color and are the size of a jelly bean.
When the young are born, the mother Hummingbird
    feeds them on tiny insects dipped in a sauce of honey
Father Hummingbird takes no care of the babies.
He likes to sit on a near-by branch
    and preen his beautiful feathers.

Springtime and Mud Nests

Springtime is nest-building time.

In the spring some birds like to use mud
to build their nests.

THE ROBIN

The Robin is one of the birds that likes mud.

Each Robin chooses a spot where there is no neighbor.

There Mother Robin begins to build,
using mud, twigs, and grasses.

If a neighbor comes to meddle,
Father Robin will drive him away.

He will let no other Robin come near his land.

For nest-building time is very important
and a busy bird
does not like
intruders.

The Robin may build her nest
   on the end of a limb
   six feet or more from the ground.

Sometimes she will build it low
   near the trunk of the tree,
   or in a vine, or in a bush.

She will even build it on a narrow ledge,
   like a window sill,
   or the top of a shutter,
   or a doorstep.

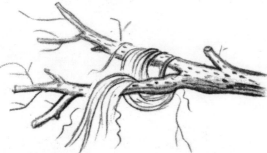

It takes hundreds of trips
   to get the materials for a nest.
First, the bird lays a foundation
   of grasses and stubble.

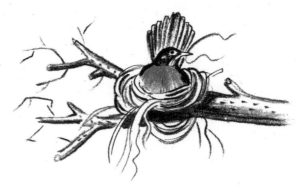

She stamps on these grasses
   to flatten them, and presses on them
   with her breast to shape them.

Then the bird adds mud and stamps it
   into the grasses, and presses on it,
   twisting and turning until
   a saucer-shaped cup begins to form.

Then come the walls.
More grasses and more mud are added
   and worked into shape in the same way
Then the bird lines the nest
   with finer grasses.

When the nest is done, Mother Robin
   will lay her greenish-blue eggs in it.

Robins have at least two families a year,
    and sometimes three.
That is why there are so many Robins.
If the rain washes the mud off their nest
    the mother repairs it with new mud.
If the nest crumbles away she will build a new one.
The mother bird will lay three to five eggs
    for each new brood.
As many little birds will hatch out of these eggs.
By the end of the season the parents will have had
    ten or fifteen young ones to feed.
It takes a lot of worms
    to feed all these hungry little birds.

THE
WOOD THRUSH

The Wood Thrush lives in the woodlands.

It builds its nest there, in a bush or in a low tree,

    near a swamp or a stream.

Sometimes a Wood Thrush will leave its woodland home

    and settle in a city or a village.

There it will live in the city park or in thick bushes near a house.

It will build its nest in the park shrubs

    with twigs, grasses, and mud from the park pond.

It will gather papers from the park lawns and use them for its nest.

The song of the Wood Thrush sounds like someone playing the flute.

THE
BARN SWALLOW

The Barn Swallow makes its nest of mud and straw.

As many as one hundred families often live in the same barn.

The rafters are covered with nests.

The Barn Swallows can even attach them to a nail

    or peg on the smooth wall.

Both Mother and Father Barn Swallow work

    a week or more to build their nest.

They begin at daybreak and work till dark.

Each tiny piece of mud must be carried in the swallow's bill.

The nest is then lined with soft feathers.

When the young birds are hatched, the air is filled with

    flying birds catching insects for the babies.

Birds That Build With Twigs

Some of our finest birds have homes made of twigs.
The twigs blend with the tree or thicket
   in which the bird nest is built.
This hides the nest from view.
   (It is a kind of camouflage.)

THE CATBIRD

   Catbirds build their twig nests in briar patches
      or thick bushes.
   They like to hide carefully
      their deep greenish-blue eggs.

THE
ROSE-BREASTED
GROSBEAK

This bird builds her frail nest of twigs and lines it
    with fine roots or pine needles.
It can be found in the woods near lakes or streams.
The male in his bright red bib sings often to his
    dull-colored mate while she sits on the eggs.
Both parents feed the young birds.
They like potato bugs best
    and so do their babies.

A PAIR OF CARDINALS

THE
SCARLET
TANAGER

Tanagers build a flat, thin nest of twigs and bark.

It is balanced on a small branch of a tree.

The twigs are piled together so loosely

    that, from the ground, the eggs may be seen through the holes.

        The Scarlet Tanager is called the Firebird

        because of its bright feathers.

        He is as bright as a traffic light

        against the dark, green forest.

ON THEIR TWIG NEST

THE
MOURNING DOVE

The Mourning Dove was given its name

    because of its soft mournful call, "Coo, oo, oo, oo."

It looks very much like its close cousin, the Pigeon.

The Mourning Dove's nest is a loose, flat pile of twigs.

It is so flimsy the wind blows right through it.

It has a few stray straws on top for a lining.

A nest like that can serve only a very small family.

So the Mourning Dove lays only two pure white eggs in it.

But these birds may raise three families in one summer.

THE
MOCKINGBIRD

The Mockingbird is the King of Song.

He can sing the song of any bird, and his imitation

   is more melodious than the original.

He can copy the sound of a musical instrument.

He can mimic a dog or cat.

He can whistle and he can crow.

This musical bird's nest is large and bulky.

It is built of twigs and lined

   with grasses and rootlets.

It may be in a tree, bush, or bramble patch.

Birds That Use Grasses

A bird can build a very snug nest with grasses and weeds.

Passers-by will not notice it because it looks like

the grasses that grow about it.

THE MEADOWLARK

The Meadowlark on the opposite page builds its nest

on the ground in clumps of grass or weeds.

It bends grasses over the top of the nest

so it cannot be seen from above.

It builds the entrance at the side.

The Field Sparrow

THE
MEADOWLARK

When the bird leaves its nest it creeps through the grasses

until it is quite a distance away. Then it flies.

It returns to the nest carefully along the same paths.

As the bird does this day after day,

a grassy tunnel is formed. There may be

several of these secret paths

leading to the nest.

THE
FIELD SPARROW

The bird on its nest
close to the ground
in a bushy meadow.

THE
NORTHERN
YELLOW-THROAT WARBLER

The Northern Yellow-throat also builds its nest
　　close to the ground.
It is very well hidden, usually in a grass clump
　　or thick weeds.
It is very bulky, made of coarse grasses and dead leaves.
It is lined with finer grasses.
The nest is apt to be found in swampy thickets
　　or in dense undergrowth near water.
The black-masked male sometimes flies straight up in the air.
　　as he sings, "Whitchety, whitchety."
Then he dives back to the ground.
He does this very near the nest where his mate
　　is sitting on the pinkish eggs.

THE
YELLOW WARBLER

This yellow bird sings
    all day to his mate.
He flies from one perch
    to another, singing from each.
Some place near, his mate
    is gathering plant down.
This material makes the nest
    look silvery in the sun.
She will build it in the crotch
    of a tree or bush.
The yellow warbler is one bird
    that will not take care
    of a strange egg.
It will build a new nest instead
    and lay a new set of eggs.

THE
GOLDFINCH

This bird is called
    the Wild Canary because
    of its bell-like song.
It is also called
    the Thistle Bird.
The Goldfinch builds her nest
    late in the summer.
It is made of grass fibers
    lined with thistle-down.
On this soft bed Mrs. Goldfinch
    lays her blue-white eggs.
When the young are grown
    they join a group of other Goldfinches.
They twitter together as they fly overhead.

THE
TOWHEE

The Towhee is sometimes called the Ground Robin.

It nests on the ground, usually in a thicket.

The nest is built of coarse grasses and is strengthened

    with strips of bark, stems, or twigs.

Mrs. Towhee builds the nest, but her mate

    helps care for the young birds.

In the picture he is feeding a juicy grub to his small son.

He finds their dinner by scratching

    under dead leaves and undergrowth.

THE
OVEN-BIRD

The Oven-bird is often called the Teacher Bird

because it calls, "Teacher, teacher, teacher"

in a very loud voice.

This bird likes best woodland country.

There it nests on the ground, well hidden

by the growth of the forest floor.

The bulky nest is built of grasses and dead leaves.

It is covered on the top.

The entrance is at the side, like an oven.

Both parents work together to build the nest

and feed the young birds.

Birds
That Like
To Use Hair

Many small birds like to use hair in their nests
   for the eggs of small birds break easily
   and need the protection of a nest that is soft.
But hair is hard to find, so it is used most
   to make a soft lining.

THE CHIPPING SPARROW

The Chipping Sparrow in the picture
   is often called the Hair Bird.
For Mother Chippy likes to line her nest deeply
   with horsehair if she can.
She uses small twigs and rootlets
   for the outside.
She saves the long strands of horsehair to
   wrap around the inside as a soft cushion
   for her tiny eggs.

THE
SONG SPARROW

The Song Sparrow is one of our most common birds.

His song is one of the first signs of spring.

He sings hour after hour from the top of a tree or bush.

Below, in a thicket or under a clump of grass,

    is his well-hidden nest.

It is apt to be on or near the ground

    and is made mostly of dead grass.

It is often lined with hair.

THE
VESPER SPARROW

In the early evening the song of the Vesper Sparrow

can be heard across the meadows.

For this bird likes best open country

such as fields, meadows, or pastures.

The nest is usually sunk in a little hollow in the earth.

It looks like a small grass cup, the rim of which

is level with the ground. The nest

is sometimes lined with hair.

The
Snow Bunting

The
Downy
Woodpecker

The
Chickadee

The
Blue Jay

The
White-throated
Sparrow

O B I R D S   T H A T M A Y B E

The
White-breasted
Nuthatch

The
Junco

The Red-breasted
Nuthatch

The
Cardinal

The
Tree Sparrow

The Tufted
Titmouse

SEEN IN THE SNOW

THE
PRAIRIE HORNED LARK

The Prairie Horned Lark is one of the first birds
   to build its nest.
Even before the snow has left the ground
   the female will be carrying nesting material.
The nest is on the ground in open meadows,
   usually in a little hollow.
It is built of grasses lined with finer grass or feathers.
Often a late March snowstorm will almost
   bury the nest and the brooding Mother Lark.
Later in the year these birds may raise another family.

THE
JUNCO

The Junco is called the Snowbird.

It will feed on bread crumbs outdoors all winter.

It does not like warm weather, so in the spring

    it goes North to nest.

Some Juncos go high into the mountains of New Hampshire.

Others go even farther North into Canada.

Their nest is on the ground—sometimes under

    an overhanging rock or upturned tree root.

It is made of grasses, roots, and bark

    and is often lined with hair.

Birds That Nest in Holes

Some birds are not willing to work hard

    carrying material for a home.

Such a bird will look for a hole in an old tree.

Or it will dig a hole in soft, rotted wood.

THE FLICKER

    The Flickers in the picture are raising their family

        in a hole they dug in a dead tree.

    Some of the chips fall into the hole and make a bed for the eggs.

    There can be as many as nine youngsters in one hole.

    To scare people away they make a buzzing noise.

    It sounds like a swarm of bees.

THE
RED-HEADED
WOODPECKER

This bird digs a hole
in a tree or in a stump.
The entrance is just big enough
to let the bird in or out. The cavity is a foot or more deep.
The eggs at the bottom of the hole are white.

THE
WHITE-BREASTED
NUTHATCH

The bird clings
upside down
to the side of the tree
by its hole nest.

THE
CHICKADEE

The Chickadee also nests in a tree hole.

If it finds a good one it will use it.

Otherwise it chips out its own hole

in soft, dead wood

with its small, sharp bill.

Then it lines this with warm materials

such as feathers, wool, hair, or moss.

It will carry away all the wood chips

that might show where the nest is.

Chickadees like birch trees for their nests.

The
House Wren

The
Tree   Swallow

The
Flicker

BIRD HOUSES AND BIRDS

The
Great Crested
Flycatcher

The
Screech
Owl

The
Bluebird

The
Purple
Martin

THAT WILL LIVE IN THEM

THE
HOUSE WREN

Mr. Wren is a cheerful workman.

He sings as he builds nests.

He likes birdhouses but has

    even built a nest in the pocket

    of clothes hanging on the line.

His mate likes to build, too,

    so she throws out his nest

    and starts a new one herself.

The nest is made of small twigs

    and lined with soft material

    such as plant down or dog hair.

THE
TREE SWALLOW

Many Tree Swallows will nest
    close together if there are
    enough houses for them.
Mrs. Tree Swallow collects
    plant stems and grasses.
She pokes these through
    the small entrance of the house.
She lines this simple nest with white feathers
    that she picks out of the air while flying by.
Her mate sits on the roof and calls to her,
    "Hurry-up, hurry-up."

Birds That Nest in Holes in the Ground

Once upon a time birds lived in caves.

It was dark in the caves, and enemies could not find them.

Some birds still build their homes in caves

   or under the ground for the same reason.

THE KINGFISHER

The Kingfisher digs a hole in the steep side

   of a bank by a stream.

It is about two feet deep and slants upward

   so water will run out.

These birds like to sit on a high perch

   over the water, ready to dive

   for a fish as it swims by.

The Parasite Bird

THE COWBIRD

The Cowbird is a lazy bird.

It never builds a home of its own.

Nor does it feed its own young.

It lays its egg in another bird's home.

The young Cowbird generally hatches first

and so gets the best of the food.

The young Cowbird grows bigger and faster

than the other young birds.

It often pushes the other babies out of the nest

because the foster parents can't tell it from their own.

In the picture a male Northern Yellow-throat

is busy feeding its foster child.

Suspended Nests

THE BALTIMORE ORIOLE

The nest of the Baltimore Oriole hangs like a basket
    from the branch of an elm tree.
It is graceful, yet sturdy.
It is beautiful, yet useful.
It sways gently in the winds, and after a tempest
    it will hang safely on its support.

The Oriole first selects
    a place to build.
Mrs. Oriole will drop long grasses
    or other fibers over the twigs
    and bind them to their support.
When she has enough long strands
    of material hanging down she will start
    to weave them together.

She will work in more branches
    until the shape of the nest
    begins to form.
The walls will still be thin.
She has to weave in
    all the long trailing ends of grass.
Sometimes Mrs. Oriole
    will hang upside down on the outside
    of the nest while she works.

Sometimes she will go inside
    and pull the grass ends through
It takes thousands of stitches
    to make the nest strong.

THE
RED-EYED VIREO

A Vireo nest is an attractive little basket

    hung in a fork between two twigs.

Sometimes the Vireo builds it in a shrub

    as low as four feet from the ground.

Sometimes it is high up in a tree.

It may be in a forest, or even in a city park.

The outside of the nest is made from strong materials.

Here the Vireo uses tough grasses, shreds of bark,

    leaves, lichens, and paper from the wasp's nest.

The inside is lined with soft material such as down,

    hair, or silken grasses.

A Vireo nest is strong and durable, and the Vireo

    may use its materials for a new one next year.

THE RED-WINGED BLACKBIRD

Red-wings like to make
    their nest near the water.
They feed their young on grubs
    found in marshy places.
They will also fly nearly a mile
    to meadows for different food.
The nest is firmly laced to
    small bushes or reed stems.
Sometimes it hangs
    right over the water.
It is woven of dead marsh grass,
    and is lined with finer grasses.

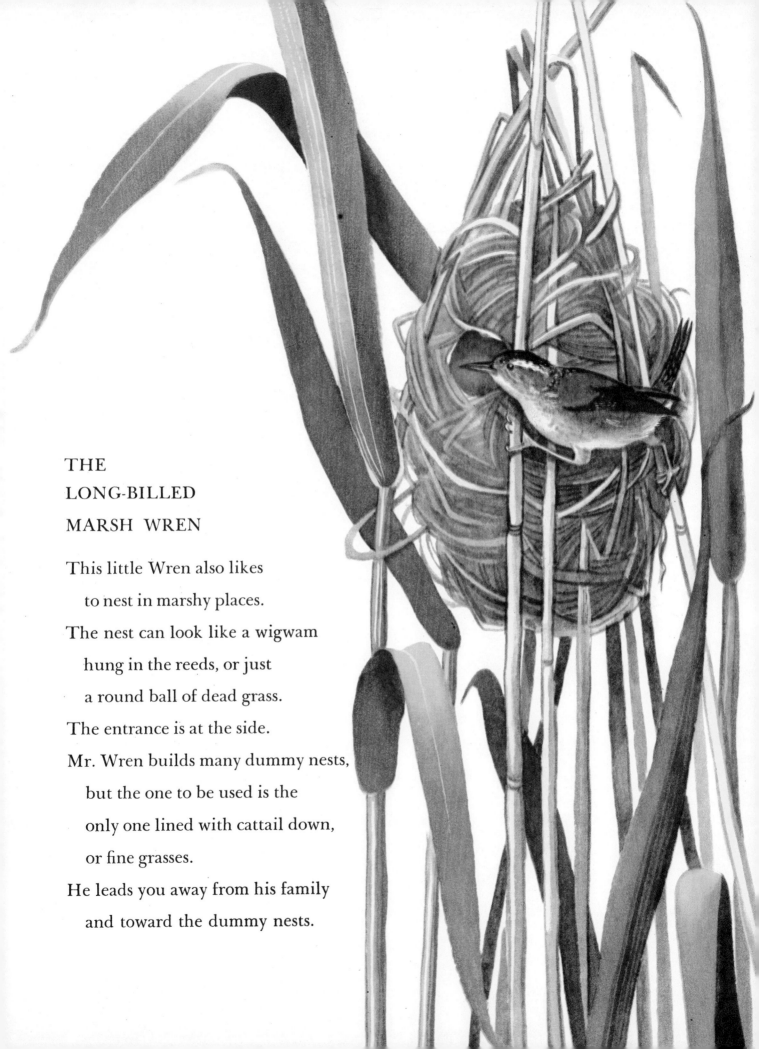

THE
LONG-BILLED
MARSH WREN

This little Wren also likes
    to nest in marshy places.
The nest can look like a wigwam
    hung in the reeds, or just
    a round ball of dead grass.
The entrance is at the side.
Mr. Wren builds many dummy nests,
    but the one to be used is the
    only one lined with cattail down,
    or fine grasses.
He leads you away from his family
    and toward the dummy nests.

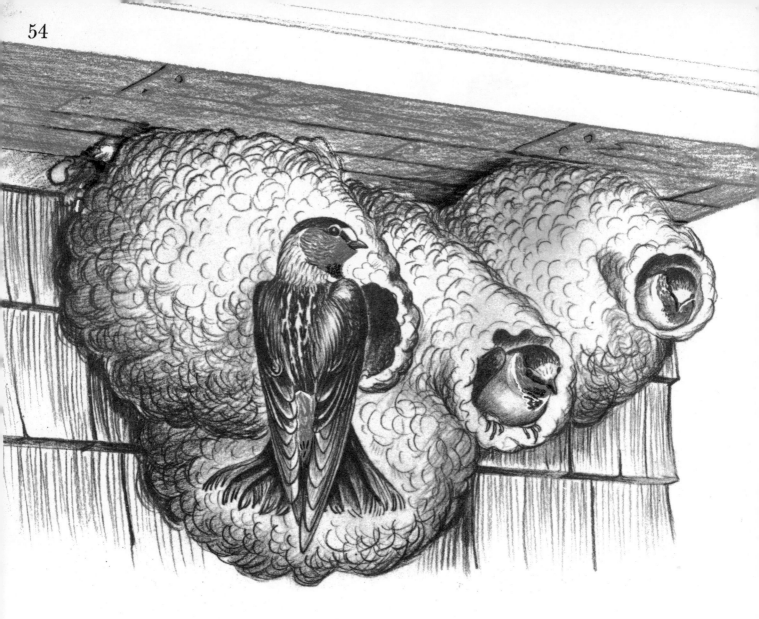

THE
CLIFF SWALLOW

Cliff Swallows nest together in colonies.

They attach their nests to the side of a cliff

   or under the eaves of an old building.

They are made of clay or mud and look like wasps' nests.

The Swallows line them with soft grasses or feathers.

Some of these nests are so strong they last for years.

The birds come back to them every season.

Others are so weak that they crumple to pieces in the rain.

THE
CHIMNEY SWIFT

The Chimney Swift builds its nest in a chimney.

That is how the bird got its name.

As it builds, it clings to the wall with its sharp claws.

Its pointed tail feathers held against the chimney act as a prop.

The Chimney Swift builds a nest of small twigs.

It glues them to the wall with saliva.

This nest is just a bunch of little sticks

    glued together, but it is stronger than it looks.

The young Swifts soon leave the nest and cling to the wall

    of the chimney until they are strong enough to fly.

Later in the year hundreds of these birds

    will roost together in the same chimney.

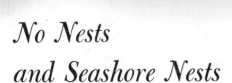

No Nests
and Seashore Nests

Seashore birds seem like play birds.

They splash in the waters and dive through the waves.

They chase the fish and ride on the whitecaps.

They do not take the time to build large nests.

A slight hollow in the sand is good enough.

THE COMMON TERN

Some birds, like the Common Tern on the opposite page,

line this hollow with grasses.

Others line theirs with sea shells or pebbles.

Some do not even bother to line them at all.

THE
COMMON TERN

Common Terns do not mind near neighbors,

    so they make their nests close together.

These nests are often on sandy beaches near the ocean

    or on islands in the sea.

For the Terns feed on fish.

The mother Tern scrapes out a hollow in the sand

    by turning around and around.

She presses her body against the bottom and the sides.

Then she brings grass, seaweed, or other drift

    for a lining.

Sometimes enough lining is piled on

    to cover the entire nest.

The parents try to frighten people away

    by diving at them from above like a dive bomber.

THE
BLACK SKIMMER

The Black Skimmer nests on open sand areas near the beach

often with the Terns.

The nest is just an unlined hollow in the sand.

This bird catches fish for its young in an odd way.

It snaps up the fish by flying low over the bay

with its long lower bill trailing in the water.

A flock of Skimmers sound like a pack of dogs

baying in the distance.

THE
PIPING PLOVER

The bird settling down

on its simple nest.

THE
SPOTTED SANDPIPER

The Spotted Sandpiper is often called the Teeter.

That is because it keeps bowing its head
    and wagging its tail.

When its head bows down, its tail bobs up.

It looks just like a small seesaw.

The Spotted Sandpiper builds its nest on the ground
    in a depression lined with the material near it.

If the nest is along the seashore, the lining is
    made of drift grass.

When the nest is inland, the lining is made of moss
    grass or weed stems.

The bird is found all over the country.

THE
TURNSTONE

The Turnstone nests very far north on the edge of
   the Arctic tundra.

Tundra land is so far north that there are no trees.

There are only bushes.

The land is covered with low-growing moss and grass.

There are many swamps, bays, and beaches.

There the bird nests, in a hollow on the ground
   or in the moss.

The Turnstone got its name from its habit
   of flipping pebbles over with its bill when searching for food.

THE
KILLDEER PLOVER

The Killdeer Plover lays four eggs out in the open.

The nest is just a hollow in the ground.

It may be lined with pebbles and small sticks.

The eggs are large, tan in color, and covered

    with dark spots and streaks.

They look exactly like the earth

    and pebbles around them.

If anyone comes near, the Plover will try to lead

    him away by crying and by limping

    as though its wing was broken.

The person will follow the bird away from the nest.

It takes a month for the eggs to hatch,

but the young birds can leave the nest

within a few hours.

They run very fast and hide under a clump of grass.

The Killdeer Plover is found all over the country.

It may be in the marshland

or in the meadows.

It may be near water

or near plowed fields.

In the fall flocks of young birds and their parents fly South.

Some fly by day, stopping to eat along the way.

Other birds migrate by night so their enemies can't find them.

Their shadows can often be seen flying across the full moon.

INDEX

Blackbird, Red-winged, 52
Bluebird, 41
Bunting, Snow, 32
Canary, Wild.
    See Goldfinch
Cardinal, 16, 17, 33
Catbird, 15
Chickadee, 32, 39
Cowbird, 46, 47
Dove, Mourning, 18
Firebird.
    See Tanager, Scarlet
Flicker, 36, 37, 40
Flycatcher, Crested, 41
Goldfinch, 25
Grosbeak,
    Rose-breasted, 16
Ground Robin.
    See Towhee
Hair Bird.
    See Sparrow, Chipping
Hummingbird, Ruby-
    throated, 4, 5, 6, 7
Jay, Blue, 32
Junco, 33, 35
Killdeer, 62, 63
Kingfisher, 44, 45
Lark, Prairie Horned, 34
Martin, Purple, 41
Meadowlark, 20, 21, 22
Mockingbird, 19
Nuthatch,
    Red-breasted, 33
    White-breasted, 33, 38
Oriole, Baltimore, 48, 49, 50
Oven-bird, 27
Owl, 41
Parasite Bird.
    See Cowbird
Plover, Killdeer, 62, 63
    Piping, 59

Red-wing.
    See Blackbird
    Red-winged, 52
Robin, 8, 9, 10, 11, 12
Sandpiper, Spotted, 60
Skimmer, Black, 59
Snowbird.
    See Junco
Sparrow, Chipping, 28, 29
    Field, 21, 22
    Song, 30
    Tree, 33
    Vesper, 31
    White-throated, 32
Swallow, Barn, 14
    Cliff, 54
    Tree, 40, 43
Swift, Chimney, 55
Tanager, Scarlet, 17
Teacher Bird.
    See Oven-bird
Tern, Common, 56, 57, 58
Thistle Bird.
    See Goldfinch
Thrasher, Brown, *Frontis-
    piece*
Thrush, Wood, 13
Titmouse, Tufted, 33
Towhee, 26
Turnstone, 61
Vireo, Red-eyed, 51
Warbler, Northern Yellow-
    throated, *Titlepage*, 23
    Yellow, 24
Woodpecker, Downy, 32
    Red-headed, 38
Wren, House, 40, 42
    Long-billed Marsh, 53
Yellow-throat, Northern.
    See Warbler, Northern
    Yellow-throated